Who's making that smell?

Philip Hawthorn and Jenny Tyler
Illustrated by Stephen Cartwright

 There is a little yellow duck and a white mouse on every double page. Can you find them?

Who's making that smell?
Sniff !!
What is it? Can you tell?
Is it Ben or Annabel?